GW00726820

English Links 1

Sheila Lane and Marion Kemp

Bell & Hyman
London

Published in 1984 by
Bell & Hyman Limited
Denmark House
37–39 Queen Elizabeth Street
London SE1 2QB

British Library Cataloguing in Publication Data
Lane, Sheila
  English Links.
  Bk. 1
  1. English language—Grammar—1950-
  I. Title   II. Kemp, Marion
  428   PE1112

  ISBN 0-7135-1430-2

Designed by Andrew Shoolbred
Illustrated by Rowan Barnes-Murphy
Illustrations © Rowan Barnes-Murphy 1984,
except where otherwise indicated in *Acknowledgements*

Phototypeset by Tradespools Ltd, Frome, Somerset
Printed in Great Britain by Purnell & Sons Limited
Reproduction by Positive Colour Ltd, Maldon, Essex

Contents

LOOK!

How much of him can you eat?

Can you eat it?

pea + nut = peanut Yes or No?

egg + cup = eggcup Yes or No?

pan + cake = pancake Yes or No?

butter + fly = butterfly Yes or No?

What's missing?

In this picture we can see both eyes.

In this picture one eye is missing.

Look carefully at the pictures below.
Write a sentence saying what is missing in each one.

1

In this picture
one hand is missing.

2

3

4

5

6

Missing words

1
snow _____

2
_____ knife

3
butter _____

4
_____ spoon

5
hand _____

6
sign _____

Draw the pictures and write the complete words.
Do some more double words of your own.

What's it all about?

Look at the picture on the cover of this book.

Do you think that the book will be about:
　　Food, or
　　Games, or
　　Elephants?

How can you tell?

Can you guess the complete title by looking
at the pictures?

Make a book cover for an information book.

Leave the important word out of the title and ask
your friends to guess the complete title.

Make book covers for your favourite story-books.
Leave out the titles.

Hang up your book covers for people to guess the
names of the stories.

These pages from a nature book tell you in pictures what each page is about.

Write a heading for each page.

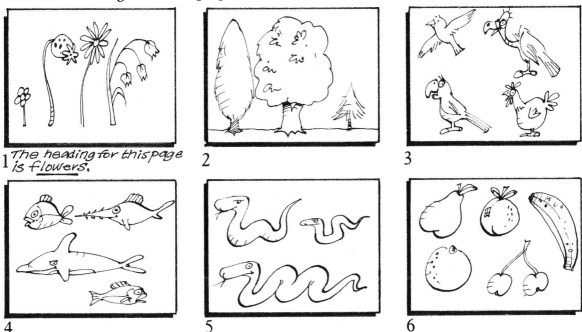

1 *The heading for this page is <u>flowers</u>.*

2

3

4

5

6

Here are some more headings:

colours   toys   numbers   names
fruits   homes   games   animals

Match each of these lists with its title and write the complete sentence.

1 Apples, oranges and bananas are all _____ .

2 One, three and five are all _____ .

3 Lions, dogs and cows are all _____ .

4 Balls, kites and tops are all _____ .

5 Houses, flats and cottages are all _____ .

6 Football, tennis and cricket are all _____ .

7 Blue, red and yellow are all _____ .

8 John, Anne and Tom are all _____ .

Who's there?

Once there was an enormous crocodile who liked juicy children to eat.

Spot the Enormous Crocodile hiding from the children.

The Enormous Crocodile arranged the branches and the coconuts so cleverly that he looked exactly like a small coconut tree . . .

"Look out!" shouted Humpy-Rumpy, the Hippopotamus . . . "That's not a coconut tree! It's the Enormous Crocodile and he wants to eat you up!"

Guess how the children were saved from . . .

the see-saw in the playground . . .

and the bench in The Picnic Place.

Guess who this is.

Trunky began to swing the Crocodile round and round in the air. FASTER . . . and FASTER . . . and FASTER STILL!
Soon the Enormous Crocodile was just a blurry circle going round and round Trunky's head.

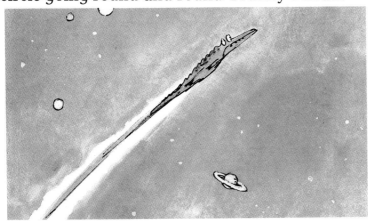

Guess what happened when Trunky let go of the Crocodile's tail.

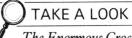 TAKE A LOOK

The Enormous Crocodile by Roald Dahl with pictures by Quentin Blake

Write *A Crocodile Story* in your own way.

I spy

The Window

Behind the blind I sit and watch
The people passing—passing by;
And not a single one can see
My tiny watching eye.

WALTER DE LA MARE

Where could you keep watch without being seen?
Think of a good hiding place.
Make yourself small.
Keep very quiet!

Write a short piece called: *My Watching Eye*
or *My Peeping Eye*
or *My Spying Eye*

A Riddle-I-Spy game

Play Riddle-I-Spy like this:
  Look around your classroom.
  Choose something you can see,
  like a pair of scissors.
  You could describe the scissors like this:

  I spy with my little eye something made of metal.
  It has two finger-holds and is used for cutting.
  What is it?

Now play Riddle-I-Spy with a partner.

Pictures of words

These words look like themselves.

Make your own pictures of words.

What can you **spy with your little eye?**
The things in these two shop windows are mixed up.

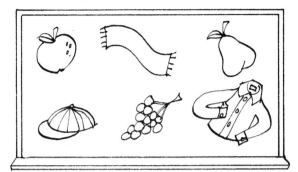 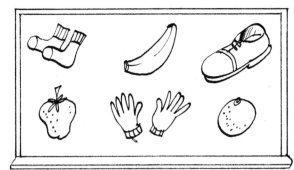

Draw two shop windows.
Put all the fruits in the fruit shop.
Put all the clothes in the clothes shop.

All things have names.

Names of ordinary things are called common nouns.

Write this list of **common nouns.**
Make a list of the things you can eat.

apple	fish	kite	pear	umbrella
banana	gloves	lemon	queen	van
cake	house	meat	rake	window
dish	ice-cream	net	strawberry	yacht
egg	jelly	orange	top	zebra

Make your own **alphabet of common nouns.**

Aa is for ___	Ff	Kk	Pp	Uu
Bb	Gg	Ll	Qq	Vv
Cc	Hh	Mm	Rr	Ww
Dd	Ii	Nn	Ss	Yy
Ee	Jj	Oo	Tt	Zz

ALL ABOUT YOU

What's your name?

Once there was a mother called Mrs Pepper who gave birth to a baby girl. Mr Pepper wanted his daughter to have at least one forename that she really liked. So the baby's parents gave her twenty-six names, one for each letter of the alphabet.

Anna, Bertha, Celia, Diana, Emily, Fanny, Gertrude, Hypatia, Inez, Jane, Kate, Louisa, Maud, Nora, Ophelia, Patricia, Quince, Rebecca, Susan, Teresa, Ulysses, Venus, Winifred, Xenophon, Yetty, Zena

Which name begins with the same letter of the alphabet as Pepper?

Which name would you choose for a new sister?

Make up an alphabetical list of forenames for yourself.

Me and my baby brother

First thing in the morning Dad said to me, "Guess what? You have a baby brother now."

I said, "I don't want a baby brother."

He said, "Well, you've already got him. Isn't that great?"

I said, "Where is he?"

Dad said, "At the hospital—with your mother."

I said, "Mum can come home and leave him at the hospital. That'll be okay."

Dad said, "That's no way to talk."

So I stopped talking.

After a while Dad said, "We are going to let you help name your baby brother. I would like to name him Tom, and your mother thinks Bill would be a good name. What do you think?"

I thought. Then I said, "Let's name him Dustbin."

Dad said, "You are being very difficult."

After a while he said, "Do you want to go to the hospital to see your mother?"

I said, "Sure." I waited for him to say something about the baby brother, but he didn't.

When we got to the hospital he said, "If you want to wait in the room, I'll walk down the hall and look through the glass at—at the new baby."

I said, "I might as well come along."

The nurse held up the baby brother for us to look at. "Boy, is he ugly," I said. "We'd better not call him Dustbin."

Dad said, "I'm glad you've changed your mind."

I said, "With looks like that, he needs a lot of help. Maybe you can call him Thomas William. Or William Thomas."

Dad laughed. "Maybe he'll get better looking in time."

I said, "I sure hope so."

(From "Me and my Baby Brother" by Mary Stolz)

Missing words

Can you remember the story?

Write these sentences and fill in the missing words from the story.

1 Dad said to me, "Guess what? You have a baby _____ now."

2 The _____ held up the baby brother for us to look at.

3 "Boy, is he _____," I said. "We'd better not call him _____."

In each of these sentences one word is missing.

Choose the best word from the brackets *without reading the story again.*

1 They looked _____ the baby through the glass window. (at, in)

2 Dad and the boy went to the hospital to _____ the baby. (eat, see)

3 The baby _____ very ugly. (looked, tasted)

Special names

Do you like your name?

Would you like a name which has a special meaning?

Angela . . . messenger   Leroy . . . the king

Brian . . . strong   Robert . . . famous

Esther . . . a star   Susan . . . a lily

Did you know that the most common family, or
surnames, in England are:

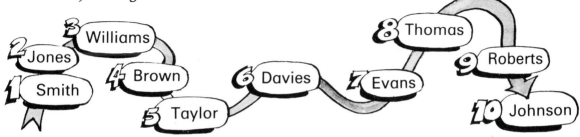

A special name is called a proper noun.
A proper noun always begins with a capital letter.

Write these sentences with capital letters for all
the special names.

1   The names ahmet, brian and clare are in
    alphabetical order.

2   The names ranjan and robert both begin with
    the same letter of the alphabet.

3   The name angela comes before the name brian
    in alphabetical order.

4   The name thomas can be a forename or
    a family name.

Make a picturegraph of forenames for all the
people in your class.

Homes

Dream homes

Once a family of mice lived in a leaky old shoe.
They decided to rebuild their home, so Pa Mouse
asked everyone to draw a dream house.

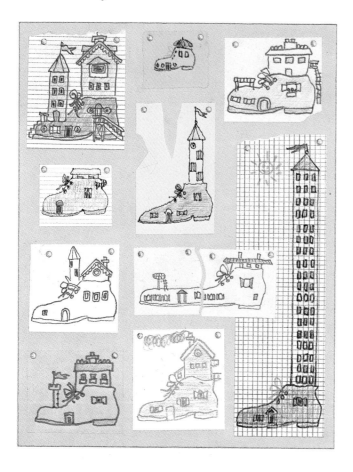

Would you rather build your dream house in
a gigantic shoe . . . or in a boat . . . or in a . . .?

Would it be as tall as a skyscraper or . . .?

Draw a picture of *My Dream House*.

Write a description of the outside and the inside.

Make a
FOR SALE
notice for your dream house.

TAKE A LOOK

*The Mice who Lived in a
Shoe* by Rodney Peppé

Where do you live?
Sometimes children make up funny answers
when people ask too many questions.

What's your name?
Window Pane.
Where do you live?
Cabbage Lane.
What's your number?
Cucumber.
What's your address?
Water Cress.

Would you rather your house was surrounded by
water . . . or snow . . . or jungle . . . or . . .?

Would you rather live with . . .

a pony in a stable . . .   . . . or a bird in a cage?

Write a piece called *I'd rather be . . .*

You could say how you feel about your name.

Where would you rather live?
Do you sometimes wish that everything was
quite different?

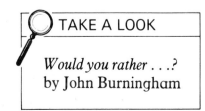

TAKE A LOOK

Would you rather . . .?
by John Burningham

Ordinary names
All things have names.

1 Write the names of these ten ordinary things.
They are all common nouns beginning with
letter **B**.

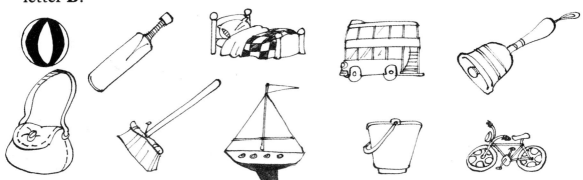

2 Now write the names of ten common nouns
beginning with letter **C**.

3 These common nouns are names of baby animals:

puppy   kitten   tadpole   calf   lamb   piglet

Complete these sentences with the right word.

a   A baby cat is called a _____.

b   A baby pig is called a _____.

c   A baby dog is called a _____.

d   A baby cow is called a _____.

e   A baby frog is called a _____.

f   A baby sheep is called a _____.

A puzzle

Write these animals' names the right way round.

woc   tac   tibbar   bmal   peehs

yeknod   kcud   taog   kcihc   esoog

Places

Naming places

A man called Mr Mell made a list of true names
of places which begin with numbers.

One Man's Pass . . . in Ireland
Two Pots . . . in Devon
Three-Legged Cross . . . in Dorset
Four Throws . . . in Kent.

Scotland	Wales	Australia

Decide which of the places you would like to live in.
Make a large picture signpost of the one you have chosen.

Write your own list of made-up names of places
. . . or homes . . . or schools.

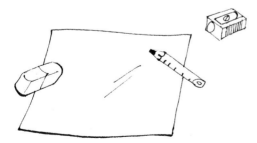

Make a picture name-plate for one of your
own places.

REMEMBER

A special name is a
proper noun.
A proper noun always
begins with a capital
letter.

UPS AND DOWNS

Up and up

A story without words about a girl who began to fly.

Look again
Look at mother's face.
How can you tell that she is surprised?

Look at mother's hands.
What was she doing *before* the girl took off?

Look at father.
What do you think he was doing?

How many people are chasing the girl?

What is the man with the butterfly net trying to do?

What is the lady with the fur collar doing?

In each of these sentences one word is missing. Choose the correct word from the brackets and write each sentence.

1 The girl is sitting ——— a branch of a tree. (on, out)

2 Two birds are perched ——— her. (beside, inside)

3 A man, ——— a butterfly net, is climbing the tree. (without, with)

4 He is hoping to catch the girl ——— the net. (over, in)

5 There are six people standing ——— the tree. (of, by)

6 They are all staring ——— at the girl. (down, up)

Just suppose ... you could fly

What would you do?

Write about *The day I flew.*

☉ TAKE A LOOK

Up and Up by Shirley Hughes

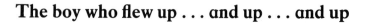

The boy who flew up . . . and up . . . and up

There is an old Greek story about a boy called Icarus, whose father made him some strong wings of birds' feathers stuck together with wax. When the moment came for Icarus to try his wings:

> He swept into the sky and away, filled with joyfulness, shouting with delight . . .

I can fly Like a beautiful . . .

As I look up I see . . .

I feel as light as a . . .

My heart is filled with . . .

As I look down I see . . .

I can hear the sound of . . .

Make a story page of Icarus in flight.

Draw clouds in the sky all around him.

Fill the clouds with Icarus' thoughts as he swept into the sky in the magic of flight.

Guess what happened when Icarus flew too near the sun.

Up and down

Up is the **opposite** of down.

a rocket
going **up**

a parachute
coming
down

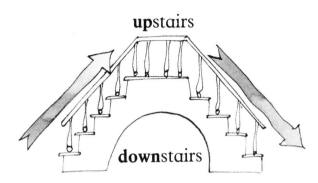

upstairs

downstairs

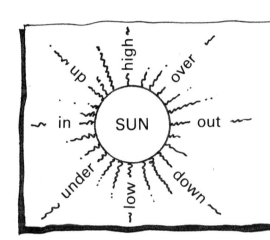

Look at the rays of the sun.

1 High is the opposite of _____.

2 Up is the opposite of _____.

3 Under is the opposite of _____.

4 In is the opposite of _____.

Complete these **opposite patterns** and make some more of your own.

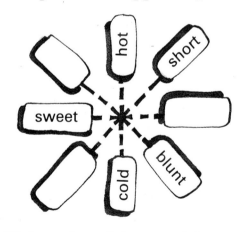

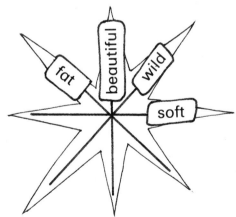

Write a describing word for each of these common nouns.

a _____ tower   a _____ flower   a _____ knife   a _____ pig

a _____ fire   a _____ bed   a _____ apple   a _____ tiger

Whose side are you on?

Once upon a time, long long ago, a nice old lady lived in a cottage in the forest. But she had a nasty family of rats under her floor.

Once upon a time, long long ago, a nice rat family lived under the floor of a tiny cottage in the forest. But they had a nasty old lady living above them.

One day the old lady went into town to do her shopping. She went into a small pet shop.

"Good riddance," shouted the happy rats. "Now we have our home to ourselves." So they ran riot about the cottage.

What's it about?

On page 24 you see the first four pages of a picture story book.

Think of a title and a picture for your own book cover.
Make a book cover using your ideas.

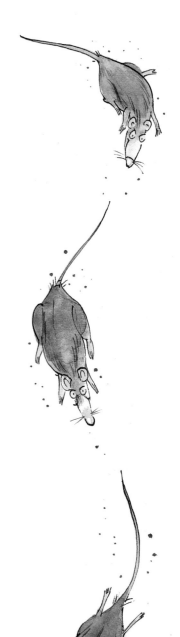

Think about the old lady

Write these sentences and fill in the missing words from the story.

1 The nice old lady lived in a _____ in the _____.

2 A rat family lived under the _____ of the cottage.

3 One day the old lady went into _____ to do her _____.

4 She went into a small _____ shop.

What do you think about the rat family?

Write the answers to these questions.

1 What do you think the old lady said about the rats when she heard them under the floor?

2 What do you think the rats said about the old lady when they heard her feet above their heads?

3 How do you know the rats were happy when the old lady went out?

4 What do you think they did when she had gone?

Guess . . .

What the old lady brought back from the pet shop.
Write the story of what happened when she got back with her new pet.

You could call your story *Look Out Rats!*

 TAKE A LOOK

Fourteen Rats and a Rat-catcher by Tamasin Cole

Under and over

The People
The ants are walking
    under the ground,
And the pigeons are flying
    over the steeple,
And in between are the people.

ELIZABETH MADOX ROBERTS

What else moves **under** your feet, below the ground?
How do they move?

What else flies **over** your head, up in the sky?
How do they fly?

What swims under the sea?
What flies over the sea?
What sails on the sea?

Here is a poem pattern.

The _ _ _ _ _ are _____ the _ _ _ _ _ _ _
               under

         over
The _ _ _ _ are / And in between are the _ _ _ _ _ _ _

Write some *Under and Over* poems of your own.

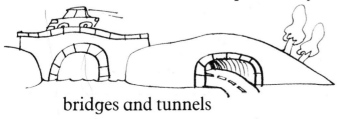

bridges and tunnels

big dipper

Read this picture poem.

Sailor John

Johnny was a sailor lad who sailed the salty sea.
He loved to be on board a ship and feel the wind blo' free!

But then one day a storm blew up. The waves were ten feet high!

'All hands on deck!' The cry went up. 'Or we are doomed to die!'

But Johnny was a sailor brave. 'Don't worry lads,' cried he,

'I'll show you how to save a ship from going down at sea.'

Now read Sailor John again. This
time make your head go up and
down to match the words. Did you
feel seasick?

SPIKE MILLIGAN

Word ball games
Toss up the letters of the word
upstairs
and see if you can find ten
little words.

Try the word **downstairs**.

27

ALL SORTS

A Christmas alphabet

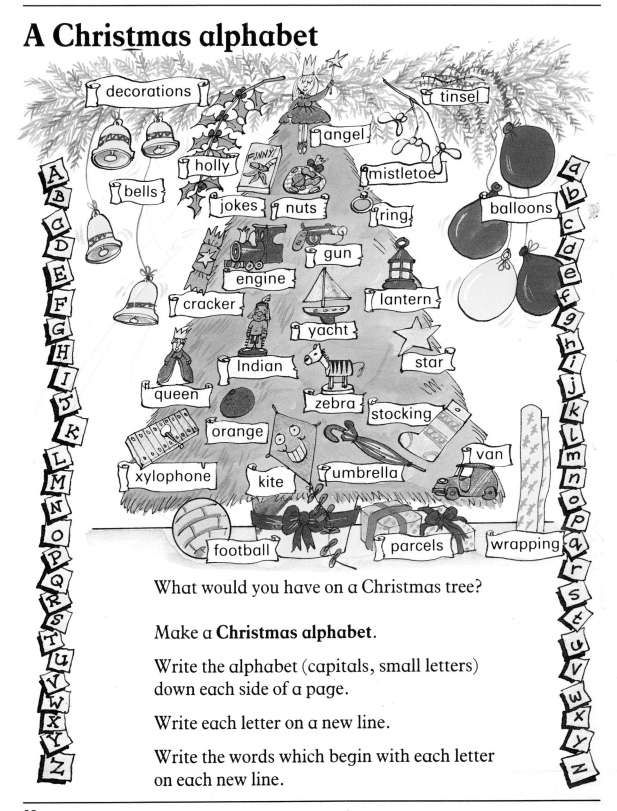

decorations · tinsel · angel · holly · mistletoe · bells · jokes · nuts · ring · balloons · gun · engine · lantern · cracker · yacht · Indian · star · queen · zebra · stocking · orange · van · xylophone · kite · umbrella · football · parcels · wrapping

What would you have on a Christmas tree?

Make a **Christmas alphabet**.

Write the alphabet (capitals, small letters) down each side of a page.

Write each letter on a new line.

Write the words which begin with each letter on each new line.

Looking at words

Missing words

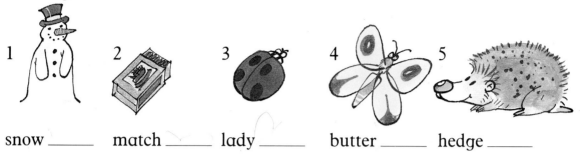

1   2   3   4   5

snow _____   match _____   lady _____   butter _____   hedge _____

Draw the pictures and write the complete words.

Make some more double words.

6   7   8   9   10

flower   light   fish   cake   baby

11   12   13   14   15

butter   rain   foot   wind   tea

Make up five more double words of your own.

Word ball games
Toss up the letters of the word
balloons
and see how many words you can make.

Try these words:
mistletoe, decorations, understand.

Looking at sentences

chocolate

£1 coin

lollipops

apple

book

sweets

peanuts

ball

pen

50 pence

Write these sentences and fill in the blanks with words from the picture.

I opened my Christmas stocking and out rolled a bright blue _____.

Next I found a bag of _____, a bar of _____ and six _____. There was a _____ to read and a brand new _____ to write with. In the foot there was a ripe, red _____ and lots of _____. Last of all, in the toe, were two small coins. The one with six sides was a _____ piece and the smaller round one was a _____.

Complete each sentence with the correct word from the box.

1 Apples, tangerines and oranges are all _____.

2 Toffees, lollipops and chocolate drops are all _____.

3 Owls, robins and turkeys are all _____.

4 Bees, ants and ladybirds are all _____.

5 Sharks, sardines and herrings are all _____.

6 Red, blue and yellow are all _____.

7 Mary, Carol and Jane are all _____ _____.

8 Joseph, John and Alan are all _____ _____.

boys' names
fruits
colours
sweets
fish
birds
insects
girls' names

Christmas Stocking

What will go in the Christmas Stocking
While the clock on the mantelpiece goes tick-tocking?
   An orange, a penny,
   Some sweets, not too many,
   A trumpet, a dolly,
   A sprig of red holly,
   A book and a top
   And a grocery shop,
   Some beads in a box,
   An ass and an ox
   And a lamb, plain and good,
   All whittled in wood . . .
   A big silver star
   On top—there you are!
Come morning you'll wake to the clock's tick-tocking,
And that's what you'll find in the Christmas Stocking.

ELEANOR FARJEON

Find the names of ten ordinary things in the poem "Christmas Stocking".
All the letters, *except the first one*, have been muddled up like this: ongare = orange

REMEMBER

Names of ordinary things are called **common nouns**.

1 top	2 srat	3 boko	4 pynne	5 bxo
6 bade	7 lmba	8 soph	9 stwee	10 tpertum

Write the correct common noun for each sentence.
Take the words from the stocking.

1 An orange is a _____.

2 A penny is a _____.

3 A trumpet is a _____.

4 I can read a _____.

5 I can eat _____.

coin
fruit
book
sweets
toy

Posting for Christmas

Make a post-box for your class Christmas mail and save postage.

Make your own Christmas cards and send them to your friends.

Write messages inside the cards.

Here are some Christmas rhyming words:

| merry | holly | good cheer |
| berry | jolly | New Year |

Write a Christmas poem for a special friend or member of your family.

Match the rhyming words. You can use them in your poem.

| star | bright | snow | hill | bell | gay |
| day | below | light | tell | still | afar |

Just suppose . . .
you received a letter like this.

Snow Cottage,
Top of the world,
North Pole

1st December

Dear Friend,
        As Christmas is getting near I thought I'd send you a few reminders.
        Now please don't
And do remember to
Would you be kind enough to
and don't forget to
        All the best till December
                Your good friend

Look carefully at the postage stamps.

Where do you think the letter came from?

Read the torn letter.

Guess what was written on the torn-off bits.

Write the complete letter.

Write a reply to the letter.

Put your own address in the top right-hand part of the paper.

number   street
town   post-code
date

Dear _ _ _ _ _ _
        Thank you for your letter.
        I'm pleased to tell you
that _ _ _ _ _ _

Address your envelope very clearly.

Father Christmas,
Snow Cottage,
Top of the world,
North Pole

Perhaps you know another North Pole address.

Riddles in your Christmas stocking

Make a big Christmas stocking shape like this.

Use a piece of paper about 30cm square.

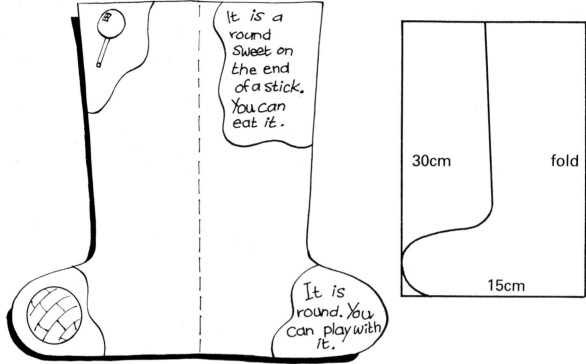

It is a round sweet on the end of a stick. You can eat it.

It is round. You can play with it.

30cm   fold

15cm

Write the **riddle** words in a shape on one half of the stocking.

Draw the Christmas present in the same kind of shape on the other half of the stocking.

Fill the stocking with more Christmas presents.

Fold back the stocking so that the pictures are hidden and ask your friends to **guess** what each present is.

Decorate the other side of your stocking and hang it up in your room.

Jokes in your Christmas cracker

Do you know this one?

Question   Why did the moon beam?
Answer   Because it saw the starlight.

Make a collection of **jokes**.

Write your favourite joke neatly on
a small piece of paper to put inside
your Christmas cracker.

TAKE A LOOK

Jokes and Fun by Helen
Hoke

Make your Christmas cracker like this:

1 Cut a piece of coloured crêpe
   paper 25cm square.

2 Place your joke and a small gift
   inside a cardboard cylinder about
   15cm long.

3 Roll the crêpe paper round the
   cylinder.

4 Tie coloured string tightly round
   the roll about 5cm from each end.

5 Shape the ends of the cracker
   with your fingers.

6 Make an attractive seal to stick
   on the outside.

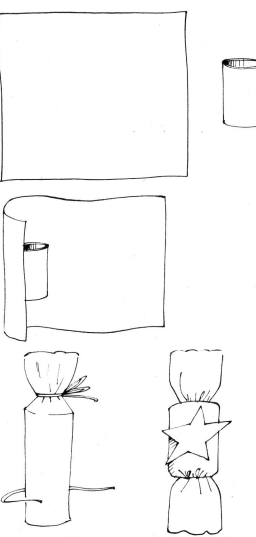

HOW CAN YOU TELL?

How's your memory?

What is the easiest way to remember something?
Is it to repeat it over and over again?

Six fat legs,
a cake for tea,
a pound of pears,
and don't forget
the bacon.

This can't be right!

Make the correct list.
How many different ways
can you say it?

Find out what the boy forgot
in the end.

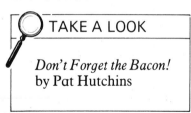

TAKE A LOOK

Don't Forget the Bacon!
by Pat Hutchins

Write this list correctly.

a bunch of jam
a pot of grapes
a pound of eggs
and don't forget
the brown tomatoes

Write your own muddled list and
ask a friend to write it correctly.

When you wake up in the morning you don't know about all the things you will do during the rest of the day.

What *must* you do during the rest of the day?

Make a list of *Things I Must Do Today*.

Read about Toad's day.

A list

One morning Toad sat in bed.
"I have many things to do," he said.
"I will write them all down on a list so that I can remember them."
Toad wrote on a piece of paper:

A list of things to do today

Then he wrote:

Wake up

"I have done that," said Toad, and he crossed it out:

~~Wake up~~

Then Toad wrote other things on the paper.

A list of things to do today
~~Wake up~~
Eat breakfast
Wash up
Go to Frog's house
Go for a walk with Frog
Eat lunch
Take nap
Play games with Frog
Eat supper
Go to sleep

"There," said Toad.
"Now my day is all written down."
He got out of bed and had something to eat.
Then Toad crossed out:

~~Eat breakfast~~

Toad washed the breakfast dishes and put them away.
Then he crossed out:

~~Wash up~~

TAKE A LOOK

Frog and Toad Together
by Arnold Lobell

What do these workers have to *do*?

a postman   a milkman
a farmer   a policewoman
a school cook   a school caretaker

Make **a list of things to do today** for each worker.

Ask your friends to guess who is talking for each list.

Days

One way to remember what you do during a day is to write a **diary**.

Write *Toad's Diary* and fill in the missing words.

My Diary by Toad

I began my day by writing a _____ of all the
things I had to do, on a piece of _____. After I
had washed up I went to Frog's _____. Frog
and I went for a _____ together.
I took a _____ after lunch and then Frog and I
played _____ together. After our games I went
home and ate my _____. Then I went to _____.

Try keeping a diary page for yourself for a whole week.

When you get up in the morning . . . you never
can tell what is going to happen to you during the day. .

In April
It is a perfect day
To be out of the house,
   and out of town,
Looking at rivers
   where trees play
At being upside down.

LEONARD CLARK

Write about *My Idea of a Perfect Day*.

Which season of the year do you like best?
Is it Spring or Summer or Autumn or Winter?

Can you tell what it is?

Monkey found a strange, round shiny thing by the side of the road. He said, "It doesn't have fur or feathers or hair, but it does seem to have a tail!"

It's not a mirror at all. It's a hat.

It's not a seat at all. That THING is a mirror.

I wonder if it's alive? I'll pull its tail and see if it squeaks.

It's not a mirror at all. It's a boat.

Of course it's not alive, it's a seat.

What do you think it was?   *Answer*   A saucepan

How can you tell?

How could the strange round shining thing look like a seat?

How could it look like a mirror?

How could it look like a hat?

How could it look like a boat?

TAKE A LOOK

"The Saucepan Fish", from *The Anita Hewett Animal Story Book*

How would you tell what it is?
Just suppose that one night, as you walked home from school, you met . . .

A BEAR . . .

coming round the corner.

How would you describe the bear to your family?

You could say:
"I saw a bear." or
"I saw a grizzly bear." or
"I saw a hairy, grizzly bear." or
"I saw an enormous, hairy, grizzly bear."

The words **grizzly, hairy, enormous,** describe the bear.

Describing words are called adjectives.
Adjectives tell us about nouns.

How would you describe these?
a dinosaur   an elephant   a butterfly?

Look around you for colours.

Can you see black, white, blue, red, yellow and green in your classroom?

Write a colour **adjective** to describe each of these **nouns**.

a _____ snowflake   a _____ moon   a _____ lump of coal

a _____ holly berry   a _____ sky   a _____ field of grass

Write nouns for each of these adjectives.

a tall _____   a tiny _____   a sharp _____   a cold _____

a short _____   a bright _____   an old _____   a soft _____

a round _____   a happy _____   a square_____   a new _____

Tell and spell

More special names

The days of the week are special
names and always begin with a
capital letter.

Learn the names of the days and
the order in which they come.
Say them without looking at this page.
Cover the page and practise
spelling them without looking.

FEBRUARY		
Sunday	·	6
Monday	·	7
Tuesday	1	8
Wednesday	2	9
Thursday	3	10
Friday	4	11
Saturday	5	12

Write the correct name of the day in each space.

1 The first day of the week is _____.

2 _____ is the last day of the week.

3 _____ comes after Monday and before Wednesday.

4 If today is Wednesday, then tomorrow will be _____.

5 If today is Saturday, then yesterday was _____.

Write these sentences correctly.

1 On sunday, jill and janet johnson went for a
trip on the river.

2 Now that robert and tom are in the football
team, saturday is their favourite day.

3 michael has been invited to michele's party
on friday.

4 mary's birthday is on the first sunday in
february.

5 The names of queen elizabeth's sons are
charles, andrew and edward.

 REMEMBER

All special names are
proper nouns and begin
with a capital letter.

Picture words

Can you <u>tell</u> what it says?

Make picture words for zigger-zagger, higgledy-piggledy, wriggly-worm.

Look!

Now read the invitation.
Can you tell what it means?
Make up an answer in words and pictures.

A FAVOURITES LIST
ICE-LOLLY FLAVOURS

First	Orange
Second	Strawberry
Third	Cola
Fourth	Cider
Fifth	Chocolate
Sixth	Raspberry
Seventh	Banana
Eighth	Lemonade
Ninth	Blackcurrant
Tenth	Lime

Write the correct answers in each sentence.

1 First in the list is _____ flavour.

2 The second favourite is _____ flavour.

3 _____ is the flavour in fifth place.

4 In seventh place, between raspberry and lemonade, is _____ flavour.

5 The flavour in ninth place on the list is _____.

LISTEN!

Who said it?

It goes in one ear and out the other side!

For the tenth time today, go and...

Why don't you listen when I tell you to...

How many times do I have to tell you to...

For goodness sake will you...

Who could be talking like this to *you*?
Read each of the balloons and finish the sentences.

Play *The Whispering Game* with your friends.

Whisper a message into your friend's ear. After hearing the message *just once*, your friend must pass on **what he heard** to the next one.

It's chips and fishfingers for tea.

It's ships sand fishfingers for tea.

It's ships sand fish singers for tea.

Who did it?

Read this verse about an unknown **noise maker**.

A _____ lives in our house, in our house, in our house,
A _____ lives in our house all the year round.
    He bumps
    And he jumps
    And he thumps
    And he stumps.
    He knocks
    And he rocks
    And he rattles at the locks.
A _____ lives in our house, in our house, in our house,
A _____ lives in our house all the year round.

ROSE FYLEMAN

What's it about?

The same word is missing each time from the verse.
Guess who is making the noise.
Say the verse to yourself with your answer in the space.
Give the verse a title.
Write the whole verse out, with your answer, in your best handwriting.

Think about the verse

1 Do you think the noise maker is someone who is always in the house, or is it a *visiting* noise maker?
How can you tell?

2 Do you think the noise maker is a creature, or a kind of demon, or a person?
What makes you think this?

3 Find the word that tells you how the house is made safe.

Rhymes are words which have the same sound, like *cat* and *rat*.

4 Find the three rhymes for **bumps.**

_____ _____ _____

5 Find the two rhymes for **knocks.**

_____ _____

A noisy story

Once there was a king who promised he would
never chop anyone's head off *but* . . .

He ruled over a very noisy court.
Everyone made a noise.

They **laughed** and **shouted** and **sang**.

They **coughed**. They **hiccuped**.

They **banged** and **thumped**.

They **booed**, they **whistled**, they **cheered**.

How many different noises is that?

How to make a noisy story
Ask your teacher to help you to play *The noisy
story game* when you are all together.

Make ten groups for the ten different
sound words.
Let each group have a practice in turn.
Your teacher, or a reader with a clear voice,
reads the story.

After each of the sound words, the reader pauses
while the group makes the sound.

The story goes on:

Now this king didn't like the noise and he
wanted to stop it.
So he thought a bit, and he walked a bit.
He thought a bit more—and then he had a plan.

What do *you* think he decided to do about it?

TAKE A LOOK

Once there was a king . . .
by Michael Rosen

When do you make a noise?
Write these sentences and fill in the missing words.

1 I _____ when my brother tickled me.

2 I _____, "Help!" when I fell off the swing.

3 I _____ carols at Christmas.

4 I _____ when I was ill in bed.

5 I _____ when I ate my dinner too quickly.

**The word that tells you what is being done
in a sentence is called a verb.**

Look around you.

Can you see people who are: standing, sitting,
reading, writing?

Write a sentence using each of these **verbs:**
drawing, playing, sleeping,
eating, drinking, watching.

Missing words
Fill in the missing verbs.

birds _____	dogs _____	owls _____	children _____
fish _____	clocks _____	footballers _____	teachers _____
ships _____	bells _____	babies _____	stars _____

Imagine the sound

Say this poem aloud and try to hear a bee
buzzing among the rose bushes.

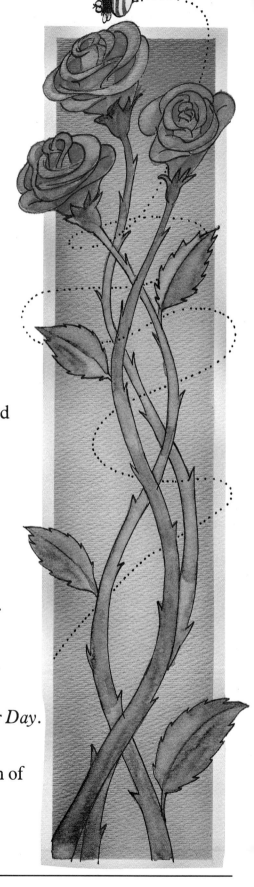

The Bee's Song
Thouzands of thornz there be
On the Rozez where gozez
The Zebra of Zee . . .
Heavy with blossomz be
The Rozez that grozez
In the thickets★ of Zee.

WALTER DE LA MARE

★thickets are thick masses of bushes

The poet has called the bee the Zebra of Zee.
The letter Z is used to make some words sound
like a buzzing bee.

Here is the poet's spelling:
thouzands   thornz   rozez
gozez   blossomz   grozez

How would these words be written in
ordinary spelling?

Imagine you are in a country garden or park.

What can you hear nearby . . . in the trees
. . . in the sky . . . over the hedge . . .
far away in the distance?

Write a short piece called *Sounds on a Summer Day*.

Think about the seasons again.
Write some sounds which go with each season of
the year under the headings:
   Summer; *Autumn*; *Winter*; *Spring*.

Which is the **noisiest** season?

Sounds around

Sit still!   Keep quiet!   **Listen**!

How many different sounds can you hear . . . two . . . four . . . six?

Shut your eyes and listen for *one minute*.

tick

good morning!

tramp! tramp!

drip

chirp   crash!

Write the sounds you can hear in two sets:

Inside sounds   Outside sounds

Jingles

How many times can you hear the sound
of letter **B** when you say this jingle?

Billy Button

Billy Button bought a Butter'd Biscuit:

Did Billy Button buy a Butter'd Biscuit?

If Billy Button bought a Butter'd Biscuit,

Where's the Butter'd Biscuit Billy Button bought?

This picture is from an old ABC book of jingles.

Did you know that: Humphrey Hunchback had a hundred hedgehogs?

Did you know that: Peter Piper pick'd a peck of pickled peppers?

Can you make an *ABC of Jingles?*

Get the message!

The policeman is using a walkie-talkie to radio his message to the control room at the police station.

What might he be saying?

". . . Foxtrot to Control . . . Over."

Mum is reading a message which she has found in the fridge. Which sentence might she be pleased to read?

This is just to say
I have eaten
the plums
that were in
the ice box

and which
you were probably
saving
for breakfast

Forgive me
they were delicious
so sweet
and so cold

Write *A Message to Someone at Home.*

Secret messages

Sometimes you don't want everyone to know your message.

Here is an alphabet code for a secret message.

a	b	c	d	e	f	g	h	i	j	k	l	m	n	o	p	q	r	s	t	u	v	w	x	y	z
1	2	3	4	5	6	7	8	9	10	11	12	13	14	15	16	17	18	19	20	21	22	23	24	25	26

It works like this:

12 15 15 11	1 14 4	18 5 1 4
l o o k	a n d	r e a d

Use the code to work out this message.

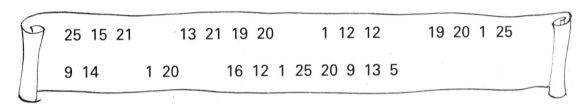

25 15 21   13 21 19 20   1 12 12   19 20 1 25

9 14   1 20   16 12 1 25 20 9 13 5

Change this message into the alphabet code.

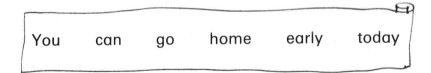

You   can   go   home   early   today

Make up alphabet code messages of your own.

Hiding places

Use an old tennis ball as a hiding place.

Cut a small slit in the ball
Slip the message inside.

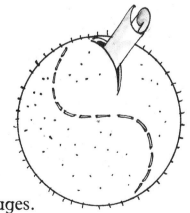

Now you can toss the message over a wall, or . . .

Think of some more ways of sending secret messages.

ANIMAL TALES

Missing pets

Look again

Find the man who is crying as he looks at a picture.
Guess the name of his missing pet.

Find the woman who is walking along with
an empty lead in her hand.
Guess the name of her missing pet.

TAKE A LOOK

The Magician and the Petnapping by David McKee

What's missing?
All these animal homes are empty.

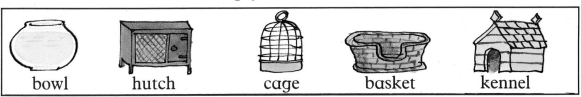

bowl   hutch   cage   basket   kennel

Write sentences telling which pet is missing from each home.
Start like this:
1 A *bird* is missing from the cage.

What are they doing?
Find someone in the picture who is:

1 Calling a missing pet.

2 Putting out food for a missing pet.

3 Painting a picture of a missing pet.

4 Talking to an empty birdcage.

5 Looking at an empty rabbit-hutch.

The pet shop
Look at the empty pet shop at the bottom of the picture.

1 Write a sentence describing the inside of the empty shop.

2 Write a sentence describing how the man is feeling.

3 Write a sentence about the people looking *in* the shop.

A funny thing to do
Find the woman in the picture who is buying a toy dog from a child.
Find the woman who has put her child on a lead.

Would your mum put you on a lead and pretend you were a pet?

Write about *Missing Pets*.
Your writing could be sad or funny.

Homeless creatures

Read this picture story about homeless animals

There was once a farmer who grew tired of his old animals.

Being wise old beasts, Donkey and Cat decided to run away at once.

Read these pairs of sentences and guess which animal is speaking each time.

> Come on, Whiskers! We must hurry.
> Wait for me, Moke! My poor old stumps feel so tired.

> It's too bad, Whiskers! Now we're old and slow . . . it's *out*.
> I wish I had a home where I could stay *in*.

> I want to sit by a fire with a saucer of milk.

Find a friend and read the sentences to each other.
Write the sentences like a little play.
Start like this:

The Animal Play   *Donkey* Come on, Whiskers! We must hurry.   *Cat*   Wait . . .

Write some more of Donkey's and Cat's conversation for the play as they walk along the road.

In the play *The Donkey's Band*, Donkey, Cat and
Dog are trying to think of a way to earn their living.

Donkey	This is my plan. We will all go into the town together and become town musicians.
Cat	That won't help us to get money to buy the things we need.
Donkey	Don't worry, Whiskers! People will give us money when they hear us sing. You've got a wonderful voice. We've all heard you sitting on the barn roof singing to the moon at night!
Dog	What about me?
Donkey	You have a fine voice, Growler. And as for me . . .
Dog	What about you?
Cat	You have a terrible voice, Moke. Everyone says that.
Donkey	I know I haven't a true singing voice, but . . .
Cat	It's a terrible voice, Moke. People will run away if they hear you sing.

Make groups of three and read the play in parts.
Change your parts round so that you read each part in turn.

What's it about?
Write each sentence using the right word from the story.

Donkey wanted Cat and Dog to go to the (farm, town) with him.

Cat said that people would run away if they (saw, heard) Moke's voice.

This is Dog saying one of the lines in his part.

Who said it?   Draw the pictures and write the words.

Trouble in the ark

All the animals were crowded in
the ark.
It rained and rained and rained.
They became very fed-up.
It was fly who started the trouble.
He buzzed mouse.

So what did Mouse do?
He squeaked at . . .

rabbit.

Guess what rabbit did.
He squeaked at . . .

Guess who the next animal was.

TAKE A LOOK

Trouble in the Ark by
Gerald Rose

What sounds do they make?
Write the second sentence with the name of the animal.

1 Who hissed at frog?
 _____ hissed at frog.

2 Who croaked at pig?
 _____ croaked at pig.

3 Who grunted at cow?
 _____ grunted at cow.

4 Who mooed at dog?
 _____ mooed at dog.

5 Who barked at cat?
 _____ barked at cat.

6 Who meeowed at mouse?
 _____ meeowed at mouse.

Animal voices
Imagine the noise every morning when all the
animals woke up and wanted their breakfast.

Make three lists of **animal voices:**

High Voices
cuck-oo
meeow-mee-ov
peep-peep

Middle Voices
tu-whit tu-whoo
buzz-buzz
hiss-ss-ss

Low Voices
caw-caw-caw
grrrrrrr
hee-haw hee-haw

Add some more voices to each list.

An animal chorus
Ask your teacher to help you to make an **animal chorus**.
Make three groups for the three different kinds of voices
 High Voices, Middle Voices and Low Voices.

Let each group have a practice in turn.
When you make the chorus, begin with one voice.
Let more and more voices come in until there is a
tremendous chorus.

Think of a way of making all the animals
suddenly **silent**.

Write about *Fun and Games in the Ark*.

> 🔍 TAKE A LOOK
>
> *All Aboard the Ark*, a play
> by Sheila Lane and
> Marion Kemp

Who's that?

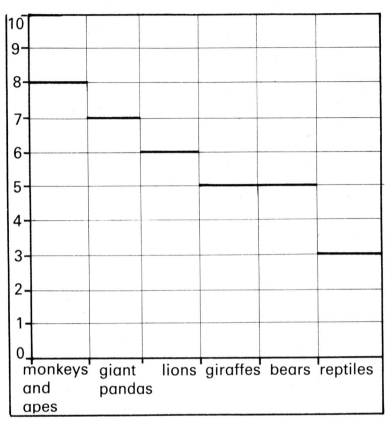

Millions of people visit the zoo every year.

Out of every ten visitors, eight go to see the monkeys and apes.

The block graph shows that monkeys and apes are the most popular animals.

Write these sentences and fill in the missing answers from the graph.

1 _____ are the most popular animals in the zoo.

2 Six out of every ten visitors go to see the _____.

3 The second most popular animals are the _____.

4 Five out of every ten visitors go to see the _____ and the _____.

5 The least popular creatures are the _____.

Your favourite zoo animals
Which animals would you go to see?
Make your own list.

Rhymes
Have you ever seen . . .

a snake
make a cake?

a hare
chase a bear?

Complete these rhymes and draw the pictures.

a _____
in a wig

a _____
eat a house

a _____
on a log

a _____
row a boat

a _____
climb a tree

a _____
wear a hat

Riddles
When is . . .

a horse not a horse?　　　*When it's a _____ shoe.*

a toad not a toad?　　　*When it's a _____ stool.*

a _____ not a _____?　　　*When it's a _____ glove.*

Do you know this one?

Question　Which animals were last to get off the Ark?
Answer　The elephants, because they were packing their trunks.

59

ALL SORTS

A Springtime alphabet

Did you know . . .

. . . that the word **alphabet** is made from the first two letters of the Greek alphabet, which are **A alpha** and **B beta**?

In our alphabet more words begin with letter **S** than any other letter. Guess which letter is the least used.

A is for April and apple blossom

B is for bluebells and birds' song

C is for chickens and catkins

D is for daisies and dandelions

E is for Easter and eggs

F is for flowers and foals

Continue the *Springtime alphabet*.

Choosing
Pick the right word for each sentence.

1 The alphabet has 26 — letters. / words. / pages.

2 All children have — toys. / eyes. / cars.

3 Giants are very — big. / small. / thin.

4 Soap makes us — hungry. / dirty. / clean.

5 A clock tells us the — answer. / time. / way.

6 All birds have — feathers. / cages. / trees.

7 Fish swim in — water. / sand. / grass.

8 Cows give us — eggs. / bacon. / milk.

9 Bees — buzz. / purr. / quack.

10 We use a pencil to — write. / drink. / eat.

Find the rhyming words
Write the word in capital letters *and* the word which has the same sound, like this: PIG . . . big

1 PIG   bacon   big   farm

2 HOUSE   hut   flat   mouse

3 HARE   head   stare   rabbit

4 CAKE   bake   cook   bun

5 DOG   cat   kennel   fog

6 WOOD   could   oak   desk

7 BLUE   colour   true   black

8 FEET   shoe   ate   meat

9 SLOW   slim   toe   tortoise

10 KING   crown   bring   queen

Puzzles
What's my name?

I live on a farm.
I eat grass.
I give milk.

What am I?

Answer Cow

What's my name?

People drink me.
My colour is white.
I come from a cow.

What am I?

Answer Milk

What's my name?
Answer Tom

What's my name?
Answer Julia

The Farmyard

One black horse standing by a gate.
Two plump cats eating from a plate.

Three big goats kicking up their heels.
Four pink pigs full of grunts and squeals.

Five white cows coming slowly home.
Six small chicks starting off to roam.

Seven fine doves perched upon the shed.
Eight grey geese eager to be fed.

Nine young lambs full of frisky fun.
Ten brown bees buzzing in the sun.

A. A. ATTWOOD

Complete these sentences with the **nouns** from
the poem.

1 One black _____ standing by a _____.

2 Three big _____ kicking up their _____.

3 Five white _____ coming slowly _____.

4 Seven fine _____ perched upon the _____.

5 Nine young _____ full of frisky _____.

Complete these sentences with a **proper noun** of your own.
Remember to begin your word with a capital letter.

1 The farmer's name was Mr _____.

2 He lived at _____ Farm.

3 His children's names were _____ and _____.

4 The black horse standing by the gate was called _____.

5 Six lambs were born on _____ day in the month of _____.

Write these sentences with the colour **adjective** from the poem.

1 One _____ horse standing by a gate.

2 Four _____ pigs full of grunts and squeals.

3 Five _____ cows coming slowly home.

4 Eight _____ geese eager to be fed.

5 Ten _____ bees buzzing in the sun.

Write these sentences with the **verbs** from the poem.

1 Two plump cats _____ from a plate.

2 Three big goats _____ up their heels.

3 Six small chicks _____ off to _____.

4 Seven fine doves _____ upon the shed.

5 Ten brown bees _____ in the sun.

Easter egg surprises

Decorate an empty egg-shell and fill it with damp cotton wool.

Sprinkle cress seeds on top and place the egg in an egg-cup.

The cress will grow more quickly if you cover it with polythene and put it in a warm place for a few days.

Do you know this one?
    Why does a hen lay eggs?
    Because it is an egg-spurt!

Write a joke or riddle on a small piece of paper and hide it under the egg-shell in the cup for a surprise.

MAGIC

What's going on?

In this picture there are three characters:
the **King**;
his old **Magician**, who is wearing a pointed hat;
his new magician, who is called a **Sorcerer**.

What do you think?
What is the king doing in the top picture?
What did the magician do then?
What might the magician be thinking as he watches the sorcerer?

Does the king know what is going on?
What might the sorcerer be thinking in the bottom picture?
Who, do you think, is the most important of the three characters?

Mertel, the witch, had given the magician a box
of magic powder.

Sprinkle some on *his* food.
If he really can work magic you will see
a light above his head, an orange
light for good magic and a
blue light for evil.

Look back at page 64.
What colour is the light above the sorcerer's head?

Think of **evil things** the sorcerer could do.

Write them in a blue flash of light.

TAKE A LOOK

*The Magician and the
Sorcerer* by David McKee

What **good things** might the magician do after the sorcerer had gone?

Write them inside an orange flash of light.

Write your own story called: *A Magician and a Sorcerer.*

Magic tricks

In this account a real magician is explaining how to do a magic coin trick:

First borrow a number of coins. Next ask someone to pick up one of the coins and scratch it with a pin, so that it looks different from the others. Then put all the coins back in the hat and shake them up.

Then say, "Now you can blindfold me and then I shall put in my hand and pull out the marked coin."

Now all this time you will have kept a tiny ball of plasticine under your thumbnail. Just before the blindfold is put on, and when you are still talking, press the plasticine under the edge of the marked coin.

Put your hand into the hat and run your fingers round the coins until you find the one with the plasticine stuck under the edge. Push the plasticine under your thumbnail again and hold up the marked coin.

Everyone will be amazed!

Can you remember the trick?

1 Write these sentences in the correct order for the beginning of the trick.

   Then put all the coins back in the hat.
   Next ask someone to pick up one of the coins and scratch it with a pin.
   First borrow a number of coins.

2 Write what you would say to your audience before you did the trick.

3 In each of these sentences one word is missing.
   Choose the best word from the brackets *without
   reading the account again*.

a   Keep a tiny ball of plasticine _____ your
    thumbnail. (above, under)

b   Press the plasticine under the edge of the
    marked coin _____ the blindfold is put on.
    (before, after)

c   When you find the coin you must push the
    plasticine under your _____ again.
    (thumbnail, toenail)

Which should it be?
smoke-rings blew The dragon  *or* The dragon blew
                                                      smoke-rings.

Write these mixed-up sentences correctly.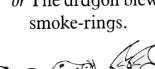

1 a trick performed A magician

2 a spell cast The witch

3 a fairy song sang The mermaid

4 a sheep ate A giant

5 evil spells make Sorcerers

Write these mixed-up story titles correctly.

1 in Alice Wonderland

2 the giant Jack killer

3 and Snow-White the Seven Dwarfs

Find the sentence written in this line of letters and
write it out. Begin with a capital letter and end
with a full stop.

     thereisapotofgoldattheendofarainbow

Magic gardens

A picture map of a magic garden

Find the signpost To The Magic Garden.
Put your finger on the path.
What do you see to the left of you?
Now let your finger move along the path very slowly.
What do you see to the right?

Move along again and look to your left.
Turn the corner and look ahead to the archway.
Make a list of everything you can see on your *right*.
Make a list of everything you can see on your *left*.

How would you tell someone the way to the archway
into the Magic Garden?

The Castle of Yew

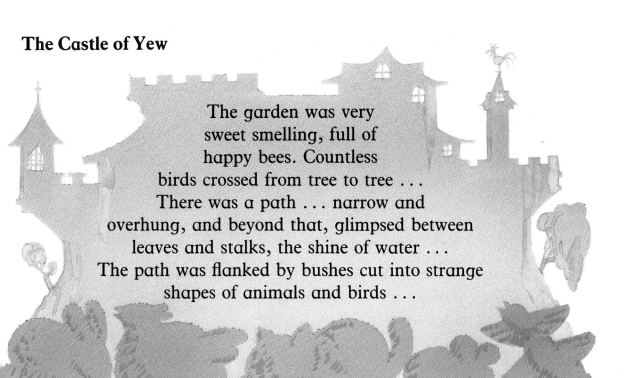

The garden was very
sweet smelling, full of
happy bees. Countless
birds crossed from tree to tree . . .
There was a path . . . narrow and
overhung, and beyond that, glimpsed between
leaves and stalks, the shine of water . . .
The path was flanked by bushes cut into strange
shapes of animals and birds . . .

Make a page of strange shapes and give them strange names.

Just suppose . . .
You walked *through the archway*.
What might you see and hear?
Is it sweet smelling?
Does anyone live in the garden?
What might happen if you touched the Great
Thorn of Sleep Tree?

You could write a story about it all.

Even if you live in a small flat in a big city, you
can make a mysterious little garden of your own
in a bottle.

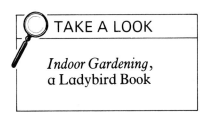

TAKE A LOOK

Indoor Gardening,
a Ladybird Book

Spell-makers

Did you know . . .?
Some people believe that witches go to sea in egg-boats, made of the empty shells of boiled eggs.

A Charm against Witches

You must break the shell to bits, for fear
The witches should make it a boat, my dear:
For over the sea, away from home,
Far by night the witches roam.

ANONYMOUS

If you believe it, you must break all your empty egg-shells into little pieces.

How many lucky charms can you think of?

You can find the names of these spell-makers in story-books.
All the vowels, a e i o u, have been left out of their names.
Find the missing letters and write the complete words.

m _ g _ c _ _ n   f _ _ r y

s _ r c _ r _ r   g _ _ n t

w _ t c h   d w _ r f

The Big Green Book

Jack found a book full of magic spells.

It told him how to make animals and birds do just as he liked.

One day he saw the family dog chasing a rabbit.

"Well, there will be no rabbit pie today," said Jack. He made a spell, and the rabbit turned round and hit the dog hard on the nose. The dog ran away, and the rabbit chased him across the fields until they both disappeared.

(From *The Big Green Book* by Robert Graves, illustrated by Maurice Sendak)

What do you think Jack's spell said?

Think how a spell could make . . .

a mouse chase a . . .

or

a little fish chase a big . . .

or . . .

or . . .

Make your own **picture joke** for two characters.

BIG AND LITTLE

Who's the tallest?

Who's the tallest man in London?

From the tip of his hat to the bottom of his column in Trafalgar Square, Admiral Nelson measures 47 metres.

Look carefully at the picture.

How many lions can you count?

How many fountains,
                buses?

Imagine that you are standing with Nelson on top of his column.

Everything would look very, very small down below.

What would look like matchstick men?

What would look like midgets?

What would look like pin-heads?

What would look like insects crawling about?

Write a story or poem called *Standing with Nelson on Top of his Column*.

Write the sentences and put in the missing words from the box.

small
smaller
smallest

1 The people in the picture look very _____.

2 The cars are _____ than the buses.

3 The _____ things I can see are the pigeons.

Complete these lists.

1 tall taller _____   4 _____ larger largest

2 short _____ shortest   5 long _____ longest

3 big _____ biggest   6 _____ smaller smallest

Opposites again
Draw an Admiral's Wheel.
Make an opposites pattern with these words:

| little | minute | tiny | small |
| large | gigantic | big | enormous |

Write each sentence filling in the missing word.

1 A grain of sand is tiny, but Mount Everest is _____.

2 A centimetre is short, but a kilometre is _____.

3 A flea is small, but a whale is _____.

4 A giant is large, but a dwarf is _____.

5 An elephant is enormous, but a mouse is _____.

Proper nouns

The name of a place is a **proper noun**.

Pick out the five proper place names in this list and write them correctly:

bus trafalgar square wembley window
london fountain buckingham palace africa

REMEMBER

A proper noun always begins with a capital letter.

Little people

I am a very small person. Sometimes people call me a dwarf or midget. I don't like that because it makes me think of clowns and dwarfs in circus acts or the dwarfs in fairy stories. Many of the dwarfs in stories seem to be either evil or stupid and I don't think I am evil or stupid! The other day I heard a young girl say to her father, "Dad, look at that little lady." I thought that was a nice description of me.

I expect I am shorter than you are, even though I am old enough to be your mother. I am not quite four feet tall, less than one and a quarter metres high! My Mum and Dad are tall people and so is my brother. Something must have gone wrong before I was born which stopped me growing properly, so I shall never grow any taller. People like me are very rare.

🔍 TAKE A LOOK

"A Different View" by Althea in *So Big So Small*

Think about the "little lady".

How tall is she? How tall are you?

Which of you is the taller and by how much?

Find the words which tell you that the "little lady" is very small.

What does she mean when she says, "People like me are very rare"?

Most grown-up people are between one and a half and one and three quarter metres in height.

Make a graph and put the "little lady", some grown-up people and yourself on it.

The "little lady" said, "Lots of things are more difficult when you are small."

Think of some of the things she would find difficult.

Think about:

● how a stick with a hook on the end could help the "little lady";

● where she would buy her clothes;

● how kind people could help her;

● what silly people might say.

Imagine what happened to the "little lady" on the day she got into an empty lift and couldn't reach the right button.

| reaching some people's door bells | the top shelf in a supermarket | the dial in a telephone box | the man in the ticket office |

Just suppose . . .
that when you grew up you were exactly the height that you are now. How would you ride a bicycle? What kind of job would you do?

Write a description of *A Day in my Life* by a "little lady" or a "little man".

Animal marvels

Did you know . . .?
Giraffes are the tallest
animals in the world.

The tallest giraffes are
nearly 6 metres high.
(That is 1½ metres taller
than a double-decker bus.)

A giraffe's baby is called
a calf. The baby measures
about 120 centimetres when
it is born. To begin with
the calf grows over 24
centimetres each day. That
is over 1 centimetre an hour.

This picture is 40 times
smaller than a real giraffe.

This picture is 20 times
bigger than a real flea.

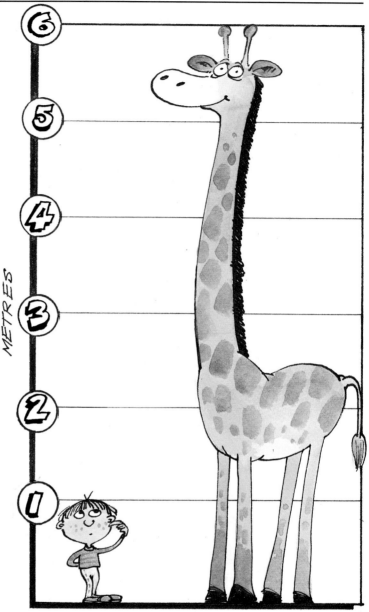

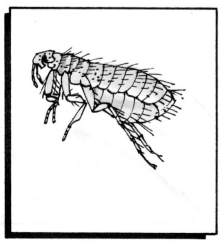

Did you know . . .?
The common flea can jump over
100 times its own height.

It can high jump 200 millimetres.

It can long jump 300 millimetres.

Can you remember the information?
Write these sentences and fill in the missing words
from the **Animal marvels** section.

1 _____ are the tallest animals in the world.

2 The tallest giraffes are nearly _____ metres high.

3 A giraffe's baby is called a _____.

4 A common flea can jump over _____ times its own height.

5 The picture of the flea is 20 times _____ than
   a real flea.

In each of these sentences one word is missing.
Write the sentences, choosing the best word from the brackets,
without reading the information again.

1 Giraffes are the tallest _____ in the world.
   (animals, insects)

2 The tallest giraffes are 1½ metres _____ than a
   double-decker bus. (shorter, taller)

3 To begin with, a giraffe calf _____ over 24
   centimetres each day. (sleeps, grows)

4 A baby giraffe grows over one _____ an hour
   in the first few days. (centimetre, kilometre)

5 The common _____ can jump 200 millimetres.
   (worm, flea)

This list is put in order of size beginning with the smallest:

   fly   *pig*   *elephant*

Write these lists in the same way.

   1 giraffe   mouse   dog   3 butterfly   ant   bee

   2 cod   whale   goldfish   4 tree   branch   leaf

How does it feel?

Ants live here
Ants live here
   by the curbstone,
      see?
They worry a lot
   about giants like
      me.

LILLIAN MOORE

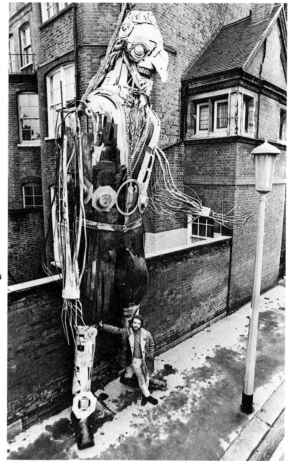

What might the giant metal-man
be made of?

What might his robot brain be saying?

He's taller than a high wall.
He's taller than a lamp post.
What could he do?

Would he worry about the little
man in the photograph?

Would he worry about *you*?

Just suppose you heard that there was a **little
something** hiding away in a shed.

Creep up to the shed with your **tape-recorder**.

What would you say to make the **something**
come out?

Suppose you heard that there was an **enormous
something** hiding in an empty building.

Creep up to the building with your tape-recorder.

What would you say this time?

How would you change your voice?

The Fly

How large unto the tiny fly
   Must little things appear!—
A rosebud like a feather bed,
   Its prickle like a spear;
A dewdrop like a looking-glass,
   A hair like golden wire;
The smallest grain of mustard-seed
   As fierce as coals of fire;
A loaf of bread, a lofty hill;
   A wasp, a cruel leopard;
And specks of salt as bright to see
   As lambkins to a shepherd.

WALTER DE LA MARE

In the poem small things are compared with much bigger things:

a rosebud *like* a feather bed

The comparisons in the poem make **word pictures**.

Complete these **word pictures** from the poem.

a rose's prickle like a _____   a hair like _____

a dewdrop like _____   a loaf of bread like a _____

a wasp like a _____   specks of salt as bright as _____

a grain of mustard-seed as fierce as _____

LOOK OUT!

Warnings

How many different **warnings** can you find in the picture?

Make a list and add some more that you know.

On your way home from school, **look out** for more **warning notices**.

Make a class collection of the signs you see and the words which are written round and about your school.

You could call your collection *Reading Roundabout*.

Make a mobile **Reading Roundabout** to hang up in your classroom.

THE GREEN CROSS CODE

 1 First find a safe place to cross, then stop.

 2 Stand on the pavement near the kerb.

 3 Look all round for traffic and listen.

 4 If traffic is coming, let it pass. Look all round again.

 5 When there is no traffic near, walk straight across the road.

 6 Keep looking and listening for traffic while you cross.

Learn *The Green Cross Code*.
Now put a piece of paper over it and test yourself.

Write the heading *The Green Cross Code*.

These sentences are in the wrong order.
Write them in the correct order for the beginning of *The Green Cross Code*.

1 Stand on the pavement near the kerb.

2 Look all round for traffic and listen.

3 First find a safe place to cross, then stop.

Complete these sentences.

4 If traffic is coming, let it _____. Look _____.

5 When there is no traffic near, walk _____.

6 _____ for traffic while you cross.

TAKE A LOOK

Road Sense, a Ladybird Book

 The cover of this book *shows* you and *tells* you about **road safety**. Guess what this book is about.

Make some more **safety** covers.

Look out for bulls

Dad and the bull

Ray's new hat went swirling under the fence and into the cow pasture. "Stay here," said Dad. He climbed the fence and ran towards the bushes after the hat. Ray stood watching through the fence. The bushes parted. A big bull pushed out of the bushes! He stood facing Dad. There they stood—Dad and the bull.

Suddenly Dad turned and ran like mad back to the fence. The bull roared after him, head and horns down. He thundered over the field. The pounding of his hoofs was a hollow, terrible sound in the grass. With the bull right behind him, Dad began to zig-zag and twist. But then the bull did too!

Dad threw one look over his shoulder, and came racing to the fence. But now that Dad ran straight, the bull ran straight.

Then suddenly the bull turned his wild, red eyes away from Dad and on to Ray.

He came roaring, plunging, thundering towards the fence, where Ray clung. Ray was knocked away as the bull shook and rattled the rocking fence.

But Dad scrambled up and over. Ray fell and lay on his back, looking up at the bull. The fence rattled and shook as the bull rammed the fence again and again with his horrible ugly head with its horns and red eyes.

Then Dad picked Ray up and flung him over his shoulder, and ran across the cow pasture back to the roadside and safety.

(From *Dad and the Bull* by Meindert Dejong)

Think about how the story began and fill in the missing words.

1 Ray's new hat went swirling _____ the fence and into _____.

2 Before he climbed the fence, Dad said, "_____".

Think about Dad running and then describe the two different ways in which Dad and the bull ran.

3 With the bull right behind him, Dad began to _____.

4 But after Dad ran straight, the bull _____.

Think about the bull and answer these questions.

5 How was the bull frightening to listen to?

6 How was the bull frightening to look at?

Think about Ray.

7 Was Ray frightened? How can you tell?

8 What words could have gone through Ray's head as he lay on his back looking up at the bull?

What about you?

9 What might you scream out if a bull chased *you*?

10 How could you warn other people about a dangerous bull?

You could make up other **animal warning** notices.

Another kind of bull

This is a photograph of an African bull elephant.

This elephant is angry.
He is sending out warning signals with his ears and feet.
What do you think has upset him?
How would you feel if you came face to face with him?

Describe the elephant's body—his ears, tusks and skin.
Describe the reeds and the swampy ground.

Think of a title for the picture—just a few words.

Write a description of the photograph.

Make a collection of animal pictures for your classroom.
Write a short description and an exciting title for each one.

Look out for . . . mistakes

When you look in a mirror you can see your face, not the back of your head!

Write a sentence saying what is wrong in each of these pictures.

The way creatures move
In these short sentences the **nouns** have the wrong **verbs**. Write each pair of sentences correctly.

1 Fish hop.   Rabbits swim.

2 Ducks climb.   Monkeys waddle.

3 Birds gallop.   Horses fly.

4 Elephants scamper.   Mice lumber.

5 Tigers skip.   Lambs pounce.

More mistakes
fish and chips are frying The cooks.
The cooks are frying fish and chips.

Write the sentences in the box so that they make sense.

1 a book is reading The teacher.

2 a big supper eats My Dad.

3 the kettle puts on Grandma.

4 their teeth clean Children.

Words out of place

Look at the spelling tree for words ending in **all**.

Told is out of place.

Told has been used to begin a new spelling tree for words ending in **old**.

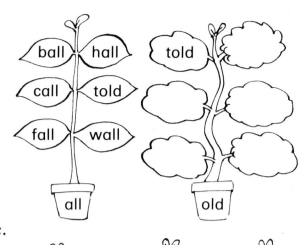

Find the word that is out of place and use it to begin its own spelling tree.

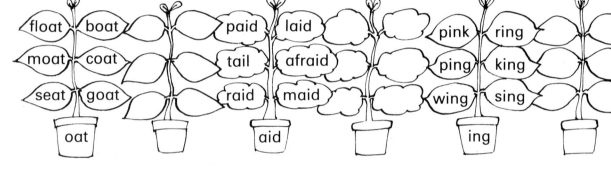

More spelling mistakes

The infants have made mistakes with their picture dominoes.

 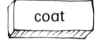

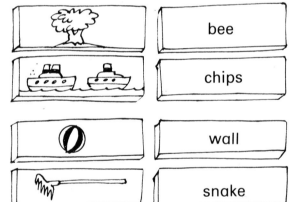

Write the correct word for each pair of dominoes, in a sentence.

Make sense of nonsense

Put a space between each word and a full stop at the end of each sentence.

1 Theelephantisangry

2 Heisstampinghisfeetandfanningouthisears

3 Lookallroundfortrafficandlisten

4 Keeplookingandlisteningwhileyoucross

5 Neverkeepafireworkinyourpocket

A strange look out!

Globi is a comic strip character in children's books in Denmark. He is always making mistakes.

Hurtigt er Globi frisk igen og indtager sin plads som udkigsmand.

Globi får et skib i sigte. Det ser mystisk ud.

Han melder til kaptajn Plum: „Mystisk skib i sigte!"

Og ganske rigtigt. Det er et sørøverskib,

som uden nåde lader kuglerne regne ned over Globis skib.

Pretend that you can read the Danish words written under the pictures. Tell the story, so far, to yourself in *English*!

Think of a title for the story and write it in your book. Write a sentence for each picture and then go on with the story.

ALL SORTS

Presents

Do people bring you presents when they come back from their holidays?

Uncle Charlie did!

When Uncle Charlie came inside our house, he opened his big tin trunk.

Inside were many strange and splendid things.

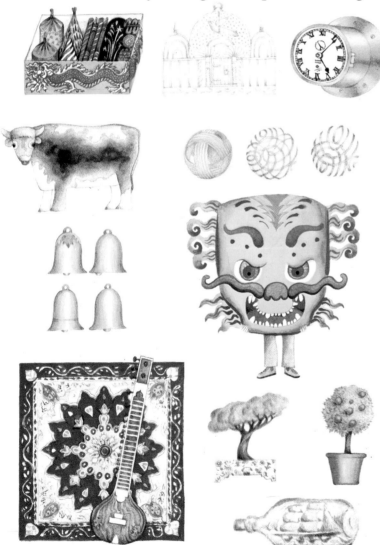

Uncle Charlie had another present which was *not* in his trunk.

It was a splendid thing,
    the best thing.
It was better than
    the box of Chinese fireworks,
    the ivory bird in a cage in a cage in a cage,
    the ship's brass clock with
    the very loud tick,
    the four brass bells for
    hanging in the wind,
    the three bamboo balls,
    the two little trees in pots,
    the china bull,
    the Chinese dragon dancer's mask,
    the carpet like a star,
    the Indian sitar;
    even better than the little blue ship
    in the green glass bottle.

Can you guess what the splendid thing,
                the best thing, was?

It sat on Uncle Charlie's shoulder and said,

    "Bless my old bones!"

Can you remember the names of the presents?

Make a picture page of the presents. Match the pictures with the presents in the list. Cover the list with a piece of paper and write the words under each picture.

What strange and splendid things would *you* put in a trunk of presents?

Make a **picture page** (with words) of your own ideas.

(From *My Uncle Charlie* by Marjorie Darke)

A real test

Now you can't see the pictures or the lists of
Uncle Charlie's presents!

Complete these sentences without turning back to
pages 88 and 89.

1 There were _____ little trees in pots.

2 There were _____ bamboo balls.

3 There were _____ brass bells.

4 There was a whole box of _____.

5 The bird in the cage was made of _____.

6 The ship's clock was made of _____.

7 The bull was made of _____.

8 The three balls were made of _____.

9 The bottle was made of _____.

10 The pattern on the carpet was a _____.

Turn back to pages 88 and 89 and check your answers.
How many did you score?

Make a necklace of ten sea-shells and colour
in your score.

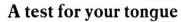

A test for your tongue
Make these two sounds: s . . . sh . . .

Say: She sells sea-shells on the sea-shore . . . slowly.
Now say it six times, quickly.

Make up tongue-twisters for: five fat fish; seven silly shrimps.

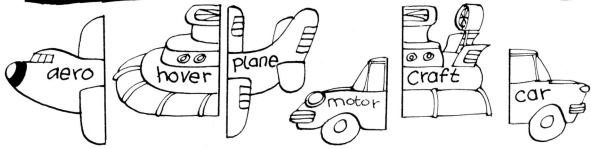

Going anywhere this holiday?

How many partners can you find?
Write the double words.

Find the two little words in each double word.
Write them like this:

sheepdog   *sheep* and *dog*

In the country	*At the seaside*
haystack	jellyfish
farmyard	motorboat
blackbird	seaweed
beehive	starfish
hedgehog	lifeboat

Test yourself
Do you remember . . . titles for sets of things?

These are all   shells

Write the title for these sets.

Picture postcards

Which would you choose for *your* holiday:
country, seaside or a famous city?

Do you remember . . .

. . . how to address a postcard or letter?

Draw the shape of a postcard and
divide it down the middle.

Imagine that you are staying in one
of the places on page 92, and that
you are going to send a picture
postcard to a friend.

Remember to write the name of the
place and the date at the top.

Write a message of several
sentences on the left-hand side.

Write the name and address of your
friend on the right-hand side.

. . . proper nouns?

Collect postcards from places you have visited.
Write down the place names which you can find on the postcards.

. . . nouns and adjectives?

Here are the names of some things which you
might see from the window of a bus:

     soldiers   fields   sheep   beach   cliffs   bus

Here are some **adjectives**:

     white   smart   sandy   green   red   woolly

Match each adjective with a common noun to
make pairs of words like this: white cliffs

Use each pair of words in a sentence of your own.

. . . verbs?

Use each of these verbs in a sentence of your own.

    playing   marching   waiting   watching   walking   flying

Do you remember . . .

. . . the alphabet?

Some of the letters of the alphabet are missing.
Write a *complete alphabet* of capital letters and
a *complete alphabet* of small letters.

A B C D	F		J	L M	O P Q		T	V W X Y Z
a b		e	g h i	k	n		r s	u	w x y z

Write *an* before words starting with **vowels**: a, e, i, o, u.
Write *a* before words starting with **consonants**.

1 __ apple   __ orange   __ plum
  __ banana   __ apricot

2 __ owl   __ sparrow   __ eagle
  __ gull   __ robin

3 __ fir tree   __ oak tree   __ elm tree
  __ ash tree   __ cherry tree

4 __ old lady   __ fat baby   __ ugly face
  __ angry ogre

. . . alphabetical order?

The words in a dictionary are in alphabetical order.

Write these sets of words in alphabetical order.

1 butterfly   ant   dragonfly   caterpillar

2 dog   goat   fox   elephant

3 David   Ann   Brian   Carol

4 Nepal   Ling   More   King

5 September   April   June   December

94

Will you remember what you did during the holidays when you come back to school in September?

Keep a *Holiday Diary*.

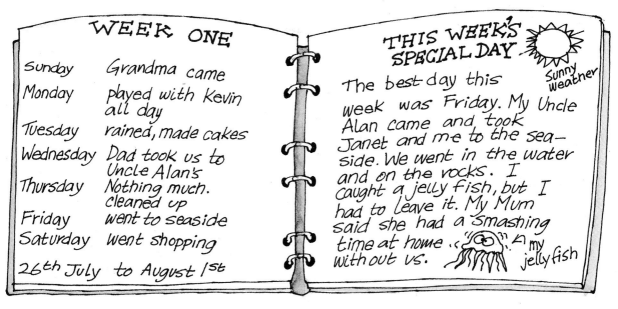

WEEK ONE

Sunday	Grandma came
Monday	played with Kevin all day
Tuesday	rained, made cakes
Wednesday	Dad took us to Uncle Alan's
Thursday	Nothing much. cleaned up
Friday	went to seaside
Saturday	went shopping

26th July to August 1st

THIS WEEK'S SPECIAL DAY

Sunny weather

The best day this week was Friday. My Uncle Alan came and took Janet and me to the sea-side. We went in the water and on the rocks. I caught a jelly fish, but I had to leave it. My Mum said she had a smashing time at home without us.

my jelly fish

Perhaps your teacher would let you get your diary ready, using up some of the scrap paper.

You could have a page for each week and a special page for special happenings.

Pictures of words
You could decorate your diary with pictures and with pictures of words which look like themselves.

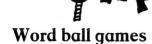

Word ball games
Toss up the letters of the word **sunshade** and see how many little words you can make.

Try these words:

football   goldfish   holidays

Acknowledgements

The authors would like to thank Julia Stanton for her help in the early stages of the *English Links* project.

For permission to reproduce copyright material the authors and publisher are indebted to: George Allen & Unwin Ltd for an extract from *The Father Christmas Letters* by J.R.R. Tolkein; Atheneum Publishers, Inc. for "Ants Live Here" from *I Feel the Same Way* , text copyright © 1967 by Lilian Moore; A & C Black Ltd for one page of illustrations and text from *Fourteen Rats and a Rat-Catcher* by Tamasin Cole; Basil Blackwell Ltd for the "The Goblin" by Rose Fyleman; Blackie and Son Ltd and the author for five illustrations from *The Magician and the Sorcerer* by David McKee; The Bodley Head for: an extract from *The Castle of Yew* by Lucy Boston, four illustrations from *Up and Up* by Shirley Hughes, one illustration from *Don't Forget the Bacon* by Pat Hutchins; Cambridge University Press for "A Different View" by Althea, from *So Big So Small* (ed.) Sybil Marshall; Jonathan Cape Ltd for an extract from *The Enormous Crocodile* by Roald Dahl, A.P. Watt Ltd for six illustrations from the book © Quentin Blake 1978; André Deutsch Ltd for an extract from *Once there was a king. . .* by Michael Rosen; Dobson Books Ltd for "In April" from *Collected Poems and Verses for Children* by Leonard Clark; Dover Publications, Inc. for "Billy Button" and the illustration "100 Hedgehogs" from *Peter Piper's Principles of Plain and Perfect Pronunciation*; Globi-Verlag for one page of illustration and text from *Globi-Står Til Søs* by Per Flynderşo, illustrated by Robert Lips; Robert Graves, Maurice Sendak and A.P. Watt Ltd for an extract and four illustrations from *The Big Green Book* (Puffin Books) by Robert Graves; David Higham Associates Ltd for "Christmas Stocking" from *The Children's Bells* (Oxford University Press) by Eleanor Farjeon; HMSO for an extract from the Green Cross Code; Ladybird Books Ltd for the covers of *Road Sense* and *Water Safety*; Longman Group Ltd, for an illustration from *All Together* by Marion Kemp, Sheila Lane and David McKee; Lutterworth Press for an extract from "Dad and the Bull" in *The Singing Hill* by Meindert DeJong; The Literary Trustees of Walter de la Mare and The Society of Authors as their representative for "The Bee's Song", "The Fly", "The Window" by Walter de la Mare; the author for the extract from *Trouble in the Ark* (Kestrel Books) by Gerald Rose, thanks are also due to Gerald Rose for re-drawing the illustration for this extract; the author for "Sailor John" from *The Little Pot Boiler* (Star Books) by Spike Milligan; Penguin Books Ltd for: an extract and illustration from *My Uncle Charlie* (Kestrel Books) by Marjorie Darke, illustrated by Jannat Houston, an extract and illustration from *The Mice who Lived in a Shoe* (Kestrel Books) by Rodney Peppé; Laurence Pollinger Ltd for "This is just to say" by William Carlos Williams; Roslyn Targ Literary Agency, Inc. for "Me and My Baby Brother" © 1975 by Mary Stolz, originally published in *Cricket* magazine; Viking Penguin, Inc. for "The People" from *Under the Tree* by Elizabeth Madox Roberts: © 1922 by B.W. Huebusch, Inc., renewed © 1950 by Ivor S. Roberts, © 1930 by The Viking Press Inc., renewed © 1958 by Ivor S. Roberts and The Viking Press. Inc.; World's Work Ltd for "A List" from *Frog and Toad Together* by Arnold Lobel. Publishers of other books in the 'take a look' boxes are: Cambridge University Press: *All Aboard the Ark* by Sheila Lane and Marion Kemp; Puffin Books: *The Anita Hewitt Animal Story Book*; Franklin Watts: *Jokes and Fun* by Helen Hoke. The following photo sources are acknowledged: British Tourist Authority, p.92; Camera Press, p.78; Denis Doran (photographer) and the Association for Restricted Growth, p.74; Geoff Goode, p.4; Keystone Press Agency, pp.39, 72; Metropolitan Police, p.50; Norman Myers (photographer) and Bruce Coleman Ltd, p.84.